THE METROPOLITAN OPERA

A Guide
by Dorle Soria
Edited by Leslie C. Carola
Photographs by J. Heffernan and others
The Metropolitan Opera Guild
New York, New York

Library of Congress Catalog Card Number: 81-86 028
ISBN 0-936752-01-7

Acknowledgments
In preparing this *Guide* the writer is indebted to the
late Francis Robinson's book, *Celebration*, and to
Herman E. Krawitz's 1967 *Official Guide Book*, both
indispensable sources of information. We
acknowledge with gratitude the help of Joseph Clark
in the preparation of the technical material in the
backstage section; also the help of Michael Bronson,
David Reuben, Catherine Mallary, Fred Smith and
Winnie Klotz, assistant to the photographer,. from the
Met and Gerald Fitzgerald, Clarie Freimann and
Paul Gruber from the Metropolitan Opera Guild.

Picture Editor: Leslie Carola

Design: Massimo Vignelli
Produced by Chanticleer Press, Inc., New York
Type set by Dix Type Inc., Syracuse, New York
Printed and bound by Dai Nippon Printing Co., Ltd.,
Tokyo, Japan

Photo credits
Photographs are by J. Heffernan, official
Metropolitan Opera Photographer, except for the
following:
Courtesy of the Education Department, Metropolitan
Opera Guild: Frank Dunand, pp. 68, 80; William
Harris pp. 82, 83, 86, 102–3, 104–5 (#1–8); Leslie
Teicholz, pp. 32 lower, 37 top, 42, 53, 56, 59, 60, 62,
71, 74; Wist Thorpe, p. 67; and pp. 106–107
Opera News: pp. 13–22, 24, 35
T. P. Dickinson: p. 23
Burt Glinn: p. 92, 108–9.

Contents

The Metropolitan Opera–A Guide is dedicated to
Andrew Kershaw (1921–1978), a devoted member
of the Met family who served as a director of both
the Metropolitan Opera Association and the
Metropolitan Opera Guild. Its publication has
been supported by contributions in his memory.

Greeting from the General Manager

There is no better way to understand the complexities of presenting grand opera than to take a tour of every inch of the Metropolitan Opera House —an expedition that might well take several days. Looking at the size of the exterior of the building and viewing the vast auditorium and stage areas certainly imbues one with a sense of the grandness of grand opera, but only by seeing everything that goes into the realization of a production on stage can one understand the skills and financing required to produce the unique experience of a Metropolitan Opera performance.

In the eleven years between the first telephone call to architect Wallace Harrison and the opening of the building in 1966, more than fifty versions of the ground plans of the house and almost thirty models of the exterior were created before the final design was accepted. Many changes were made in every detail of the house, some for economic necessities and some representing restudy and improvement. After eleven years of dedicated labor by the architect, the engineers, the construction workers and, above all, the Metropolitan's professional staff, the house was inaugurated with the world premiere of Samuel Barber's *Antony and Cleopatra*, especially commissioned for the opening, and directed and designed by Franco Zeffirelli. From the outset the house proved to be a great theater. One can always make improvements in any structure, and certainly modern technology and the demands of opera production in the 1980's have required many changes in the original concept—changes that will continue to be made for as long as the house stands. But whatever these modifications may be, the Metropolitan Opera House will remain one of the great theaters of the world. In the words of a member of our technical staff, "the house works." I hope this book will introduce you to the daily miracle that is the Metropolitan Opera House.

Anthony A. Bliss

This drawing shows Lincoln Center's constituents. Avery Fisher Hall (1), home of the New York Philharmonic, is separated by the plaza with its fountain from the New York State Theater (2), home of the New York City Ballet and the New York City Opera. In the center rear, commanding the plaza, is the Metropolitan Opera House (3). To its north is the New York Public Library & Museum of the Performing Arts (4) and the Vivian Beaumont Theater (5), facing the pool with the Henry Moore sculpture Reclining Figure; beyond is the Juilliard School (6).

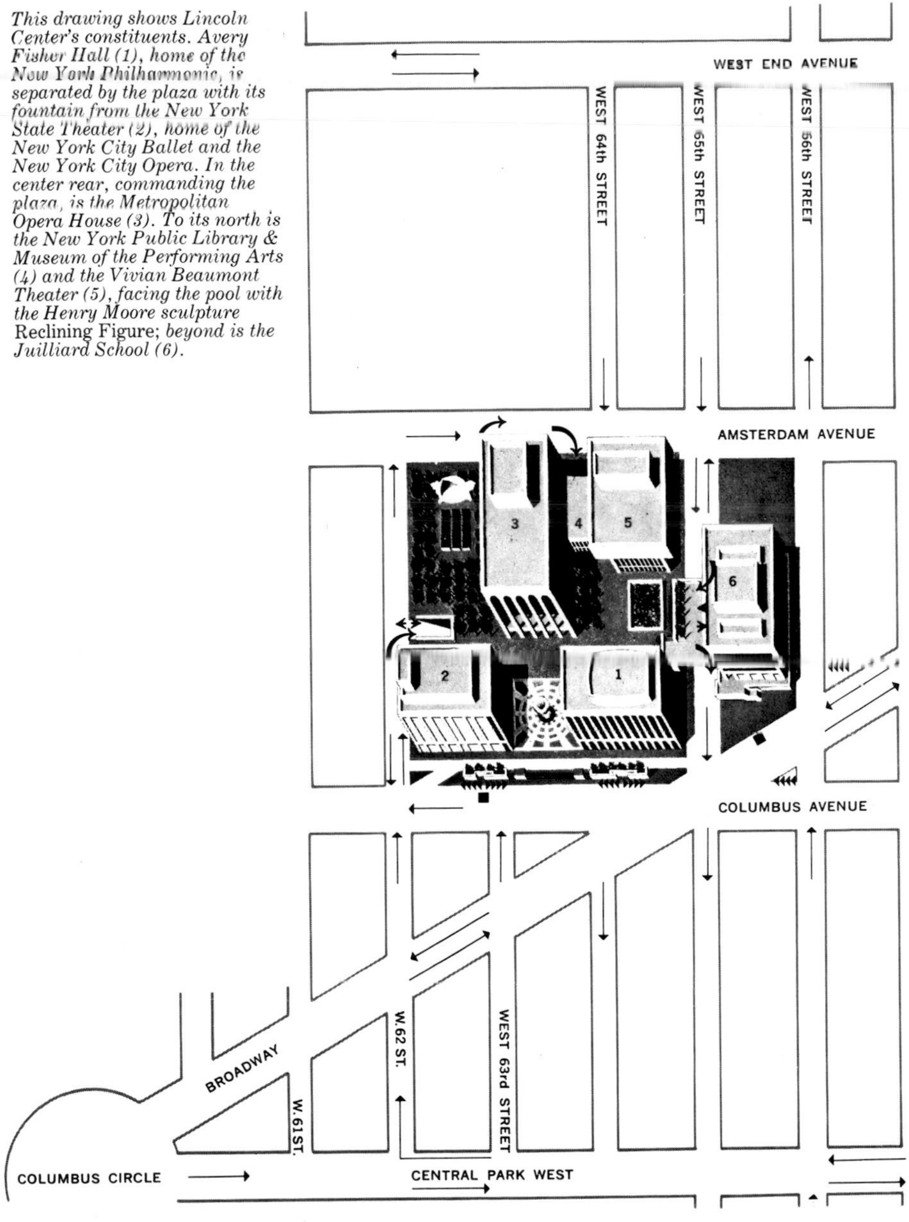

WEST END AVENUE

WEST 64th STREET

WEST 65th STREET

WEST 66th STREET

AMSTERDAM AVENUE

COLUMBUS AVENUE

BROADWAY

W. 61 ST.

W. 62 ST.

WEST 63rd STREET

CENTRAL PARK WEST

COLUMBUS CIRCLE

Story of the Metropolitan Opera

For a century the Metropolitan has been the symbol of grand opera in this country. It has been called "a national treasure" and it is a mecca which draws visitors from all over the world. In New York it is a tourist's "must," sharing interest and importance with the Statue of Liberty, the Empire State Building and the United Nations. The Metropolitan, dominating Lincoln Center, is an internationally famous opera house, together with La Scala and the Vienna Opera, the Paris Opera and the Royal Opera House, London.

New York has always been an opera town. In 1854, on Fourteenth Street and Irving Place, the Academy of Music was built, designed expressly for the presentation of opera. For many years the "socially correct" place to be seen was in a loge at the Academy. Unfortunately, however, there were only eighteen boxes, sold year after year to the same blue-blood owners. It was a period when New York was expanding, when buildings were growing higher, when there was a tremendous surge of immigration. It was a time which bred a strong group of new millionaires who resented sitting downstairs at the Academy and being snubbed by the old Knickerbocker society box-holders. And so, in 1880, sixty-five rich men decided to build their own opera house and to build it farther uptown, within easier reach of upper Fifth Avenue where, at Fifty-second Street, one of the moving spirits, William Henry Vanderbilt, was completing his mansion. Unfortunately, the architect engaged "had never entered a playhouse" and both public and artists were to suffer for that lack of experience until the Met finally moved into its splendid and functionally designed second home at Lincoln Center in September 1966. But if the first Metropolitan had no place for storing scenery, for proper rehearsals, if its artists' dressing rooms were impossible and its sightlines poor from many parts of the house, it did have one thing—it had boxes, 122 of them, and a seating capacity of 3,790. In the course of time virtually every celebrated singer in the world appeared on its stage. It grew to fill a unique place in the life of the city and nation.

The Metropolitan opened on October 22, 1883. The
Brooklyn Bridge had been inaugurated the spring
before. New York by now was a city of almost two
million people. The opera house was seven stories
high with a façade of yellow brick which Colonel
James H. Mapleson, impresario of the Academy,
maliciously called "that new yellow brewery on
Broadway." It stood on Thirty-ninth to Fortieth
streets, between Broadway and Seventh Avenue.
The first night was Gounod's *Faust* with Christine
Nilsson, the Swedish soprano, as Marguerite and the
Italian tenor Italo Campanini in the title role. The
latter's brother, conductor Cleofonte Campanini,
later directed the first American performance of
Otello at the Metropolitan.

For the first twenty-five years the "privilege" of
presenting opera at the Metropolitan was a
concession and the first to have it was Henry E.
Abbey who had been a jeweler, theater owner and
manager, and a one-time "cornet player in a brass
band in Akron, Ohio, whence he came." Nevertheless
he gave New York grand opera, spending money
wildly. The orchestra was imported from abroad,
large fees were offered to tempt artists of
reputation, costumes were ordered from Worth of
Paris. Performances glittered with such singers as
Marcella Sembrich. When a deficit of almost $600,000
resulted, the Abbey contract was not renewed.
That first year everything, even *Lohengrin*, was
sung in Italian. But from 1884 to 1891 it was all
German, including *Carmen* in which Lilli Lehmann
made her debut. From Abbey the stockholders had
turned to conductor Leopold Damrosch, a friend of
Liszt and Wagner. It was agreed that he would
engage a company of German singers including
Amalie Materna, whom Wagner had chosen for
Brünnhilde at his first Bayreuth Festival. New York
at that time had a large German population and on
opening night "the audience surpassed in number
that of the memorable opening a year ago," wrote
the *New York Tribune*. Less than three months after
taking office Leopold Damrosch died. In the years
that followed the stockholders retained their
secretary Edmond C. Stanton as manager but there
was a strong conductor team in the famous

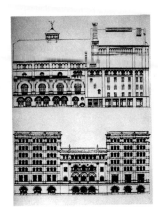

*The old Metropolitan Opera
House at Broadway and 39th
Street (photo opposite; drawing
above) was the Met's home from
1883–84 through 1965–66.
Though its exterior gave rise to
the rude nickname of "the
yellow brick brewery" its
interior was universally
admired—its rich maroon and
red coloring, its famous gold
curtain, its "Golden Horseshoe"
of boxes. Its elegance could not,
however, balance its physical
inadequacies: poor sight lines,
lack of storage space, the stage
itself. Inevitably the
Metropolitan moved to a new
and modern home. When the
wreckers' ball was to descend on
the old house, public sentiment
ran high and there were waves
of protest. But, as Rudolf Bing
wrote: "The need for a new
opera house for the
Metropolitan had been obvious
for a generation before my
arrival." In the end "there was
a committee 'to save the Met,'
but really the house was beyond
saving."*

Hungarian Anton Seidl and in young Walter Damrosch, son of Leopold. Seidl introduced *Die Meistersinger* and *Tristan und Isolde* to America and in one the week conducted the entire Ring. The "German years" ended with the 1891–92 season when Abbey was given another chance, together with John B. Schoeffel of Boston and Maurice Grau, impresario of Covent Garden. The first night opera was Gounod's *Roméo et Juliette* in its "first New York performance in French" with Emma Eames and Jean de Reszke as the lovers, and Edouard de Reszke as Friar Lawrence. *Il Trovatore* was given the second night, with Lilli Lehmann as Leonora, her "first venture in Italian."

There was no opera during 1892–93. A fire had gutted the house during the summer. When it reopened the boxes had been reduced to a total of seventy in two tiers. The triumvirate carried on until, in October 1896, Abbey died. Beginning with 1898 Grau was to be alone, remaining through 1902–03. During this period the repertoire was sung in French or Italian and great casts were the rule. There were the debuts of Emma Calvé and Nellie Melba and Pol Plançon, of Schumann-Heink and Johanna Gadski and of Antonio Scotti as Don Giovanni. The Grau era brought the first Metropolitan *Bohème* and the first American *Tosca*. It also presented, for the first and last time in Metropolitan history, a work by a woman, a one-act opera *Der Wald* by the English composer Ethel Smyth. One opera, *Faust*, was so popular that it was sung ten times in 1896–97 and the Metropolitan was nicknamed the *Faustspielhaus*.

1903–04 brought a new manager, Heinrich Conried, a one-time actor at the Burg Theater in Vienna and a man of the theater. On the memorable opening night of November 23, 1903, a thirty-year old Italian tenor, Enrico Caruso, made his American debut as the Duke in *Rigoletto*. To him went the honor of every opening night thereafter until his death, except once when he deferred to Geraldine Farrar. Conried's five seasons brought the first staged performance, unsanctioned, of *Parsifal* outside Bayreuth, the American premiere of *Salome* which so scandalized the directors that the opera was withdrawn after one

When Giulio Gatti-Cassaza (above) arrived to become general manager in 1908 he found no rehearsal room, no storage space. He was told not to worry, that in two or three years a new Metropolitan Opera House would be built, answering all their needs. It took more than fifty-eight years for this to happen.

performance and did not return until 1934, the debuts of Farrar and Chaliapin and of Gustav Mahler who made his first Metropolitan Opera appearance on New Year's Day 1908, with Fremstad as Isolde. 1908–09: Giulio Gatti-Casazza arrived from La Scala, an imposing figure, an autocrat, a man of uncompromising principles and a practical man of the theater who was to remain manager of the Metropolitan an unrivalled twenty-seven years. Toscanini, who came with him, was no less dedicated and demanding. He set new standards of orchestral playing and vocal ensemble, of dramatic and musical fidelity to the score. A reproof to prima donna Geraldine Farrar has become classic: "There are no stars on this stage, Madame. There are only stars in heaven."

Inaugural night Toscanini conducted *Aida* with Emmy Destinn in her American debut and with Caruso, Louise Homer and Scotti. In the years ahead were to be such newcomers as Amato, Martinelli and Slezak, Matzenauer, Tetrazzini, Frieda Hempel, Lucrezia Bori and Elisabeth Schumann who was first heard as Sophie in *Der Rosenkavalier*. The world premiere of *The Girl of the Golden West,* for which Puccini came to New York, was under the baton of Toscanini but the Maestro did not limit himself to the Italian repertoire. He conducted such operas as *Manon*, Gluck's *Orfeo ed Euridice* and *Armide* and the first American performance of *Boris Godunov;* he also, in the words of Francis Robinson, "helped himself to *Götterdämmerung* and *Tristan* and Mahler's days were numbered." The Maestro's last appearance was in *Iris*, April 14, 1915, after which, without fanfare, he left the Metropolitan never to return. There was no explanation although there had been rumors of differences with Gatti-Casazza; also, Italy was on the verge of war and Toscanini wanted to be home.

Conductor Alfred Hertz, a Met mainstay for thirteen seasons, left for the San Francisco Symphony, and Gatti-Casazza, for his major replacement, appointed Artur Bodanzky, the distinguished Viennese-born conductor, who was to be the Metropolitan's major Wagner exponent for twenty-four years. He conducted Flagstad's first performance and Caruso's

The proscenium of the Old Met. Above it were carved the names of the opera composers most famous at the turn of the century: Gluck, Mozart, Beethoven, Verdi, Wagner, Gounod. Gluck is no longer in the repertoire and the Met has long since ceased to be known as the Faustspielhaus. *Puccini is missing because, at that time, his operas were just being introduced at the Metropolitan. La Bohème and Tosca were the first, in the 1900–01 season.*

17

Enrico Caruso lent glory to the Metropolitan from 1903 until his last performance, December 24, 1920, singing Eléazar in La Juive. He made his New York, London, Paris, Berlin, Vienna debuts in Rigoletto, *at right.*

Rosa Ponselle made her Met debut November 15, 1918, as Leonora in La Forza del Destino, *opposite Caruso. She remained nineteen seasons, sang twenty-two roles. This is her memorable Norma.*

Lawrence Tibbett made a quiet Met debut November 24, 1923, but on January 2, 1925, in Falstaff *with the great Scotti he sang Ford and stopped the show. He starred at the Met until 1950. His Simon Boccanegra is shown here.*

Lily Pons, coloratura, did 283 performances of ten operas at the Met. She began as Lucia in January 1931, remained with the company twenty-five years. She is perhaps best remembered for her Lakmé.

Lauritz Melchior, Danish Heldentenor, was a pillar of the Wagnerian roster for twenty-four seasons. Here he is as Tannhäuser, his 1926 debut.

Kirsten Flagstad, made her Met debut February 2, 1935, as Sieglinde, followed by Isolde four days later. Here: Elisabeth in Tannhäuser.

Leonard Warren, star of the Metropolitan twenty-two years, made his debut January 13, 1939, as Paolo in Simon Boccanegra. *On March 4, 1960, he died onstage at the Met during* La Forza del Destino. *Here: Tonio in* Pagliacci.

Zinka Milanov, soprano, made her Met debut December 17, 1937, as Leonora in Il Trovatore. *She appeared 421 times with the company. Here she is as Donna Anna in* Don Giovanni.

Richard Tucker made his Met debut January 25, 1945, as Enzo in La Gioconda, *the first of thirty roles at the Met. The tenor is pictured as Des Grieux in* Manon Lescaut.

last and he introduced virtually every important Wagnerian singer of his period—Leider, Lotte Lehmann and Thorborg, Melchior and Schorr. He was to be succeeded by twenty-five year-old Erich Leinsdorf, the beginning of another long association with the Met. Others in the pit were Giorgio Polacco, Tullio Serafin, Pierre Monteux and Wilfred Pelletier. Financially and artistically the house flourished. Gatti-Casazza made mechanical and stage improvements, fostered native singers and native opera. He also continued to bring great artists from abroad. Among the Americans were Rose Bampton, Florence Easton, Grace Moore, Rosa Ponselle, Gladys Swarthout, Lawrence Tibbett, plus a young Canadian tenor, Edward Johnson, destined to succeed Gatti. Galli-Curci arrived and Claudia Muzio, Lily Pons, Elisabeth Rethberg, and there was Maria Jeritza who, after her debut in Korngold's *Tote Stadt*, appeared in *Tosca* in which the golden-haired soprano brought down the house singing "Vissi d'Arte" lying on the floor. De Luca, Gigli, Schipa, and Tita Ruffo came and Ezio Pinza whose Don Giovanni was to make him a matinée idol and who was to remain from 1926 until 1943; a few years after he was to star on Broadway in *South Pacific*.

Repertory ranged from the first American performances of *Turandot, Jenufa, Simon Boccanegra, Sadko, Le Coq D'or, Die Aegyptische Helena* and *Jonny Spielt Auf* to the world premiere of the Puccini triptych, *Gianni Schicchi, Il Tabarro* and *Suor Angelica*. And, during his twenty-seven years, Gatti-Casazza produced sixteen American operas.

1929 opened with *Manon Lescaut*, with Bori, Gigli and De Luca, Serafin conducting. The next day came the stock market crash. The Metropolitan was not, however, at first affected; a considerable financial reserve had been built up. But soon the depression took its toll. In 1932–33 the season was sliced by a third and the artists took a ten percent cut. The situation, however, had developed a new source of income and influence. The National Broadcasting Company offered to pay to broadcast opera from the Metropolitan. The offer, with some skepticism, was accepted and on Christmas Day 1931, *Hansel and*

Enrico Caruso

Rosa Ponselle

Lawrence Tibbett

Lily Pons

Lauritz Melchior

Kirsten Flagstad

Leonard Warren

Zinka Milanov

Richard Tucker

Gretel went on the air, the first historic broadcast. In 1932–33 a campaign to raise $300,000 succeeded in part because of the response from radio listeners. It was the beginning of the recognition of the Metropolitan as a national opera house. 1935–36: with the sudden death of the first appointee, Herbert Witherspoon, Edward Johnson was named manager. A popular figure, he remained fifteen years, managing to steer the Metropolitan through the dark waters of the post-depression and war years. But help came to him early. Mrs. August Belmont, first woman member of the Metropolitan board, founded the Metropolitan Opera Guild in 1935 to aid in fund raising and education. In less than four months the Guild had 2,000 members. Today it has over 100,000 and its magazine, *Opera News* has the widest circulation of any magazine of its kind. During the First World War German opera had been dropped. But during the Second World War it retained its stronghold. The only opera cancelled was *Butterfly* after Pearl Harbor; it was not heard again until 1946 when it returned with Licia Albanese. Johnson brought many great artists from all parts of the world to the Metropolitan, among them young Zinka Milanov who was to become the great Verdi soprano of her time, Bidù Sayão, Jarmila Novotna and Astrid Varnay; tenors Bjoerling, Di Stefano, Tagliavini, Vinay, baritone Singher, bassos Baccaloni, Kipnis and Tajo. But American singers played an increasingly important role, such artists as Dorothy Kirsten, Regina Resnik, Eleanor Steber, Risë Stevens, Helen Traubel, Blanche Thebom, Jerome Hines, Charles Kullman, Robert Merrill, Jan Peerce, Richard Tucker and Leonard Warren. The Johnson era will also be remembered for its conductors, brought to these shores by the war: Bruno Walter, Sir Thomas Beecham, George Szell, Fritz Busch, Fritz Stiedry and Fritz Reiner. Walter made his debut with *Fidelio* on February 14, 1941, with Flagstad as Leonora, René Maison as Florestan, Kipnis as Rocco, Herbert Janssen and Julius Huehn as Don Fernando and Don Pizarro. Reiner first appeared in the Metropolitan pit with *Salome* on February 4, 1949, the spectacular performance in which Ljuba Welitsch also made her

debut. Novelties of the Johnson years were few but
they included Britten's *Peter Grimes*, the first
British work since Dame Ethel Smyth's *Der Wald*.
1950–51: Rudolf Bing—later Sir Rudolf—became the
new general manager. Born in Vienna, trained in
Germany, he had been general manager of the
Glyndebourne Festival and founder of the Edinburgh
Festival previously. He was to head the company
twenty-two eventful years, during which the
Metropolitan would move to Lincoln Center.
Rudolf Bing was an autocrat, a conservative, but an
innovator in the theater. He believed opera was
drama as well as music and he not only engaged
leading conductors and singers for the Metropolitan
but also leading directors from Broadway and the
West End to stage the productions, and
distinguished painters and designers to mount them.
He brought back Kirsten Flagstad from Norway
despite public criticism of the fact that she had
chosen to live the war years under German
occupation. He pursued the difficult Maria Callas
until she capitulated and, though later they feuded,
he had the glory of presenting her in performances
that made history at the Met, the Callas Norma,
Tosca, Lucia and Violetta.
He loved Verdi and did nine new productions of
Verdi operas. He chose *Don Carlo*, not heard at the
Met since 1922, for his opening night, November 6,
1950, the occasion on which Cesare Siepi made his
debut as Philip II. During that first season there was
a surprise debut, nineteen-year-old Roberta Peters,
a soprano who still charms Met audiences, as Zerlina.
There was also a successful *Fledermaus* in English.
Garson Kanin staged it; musical comedy lyricist
Howard Dietz did the lively translation; Eugene
Ormandy conducted. The cast included Ljuba
Welitsch, Patrice Munsel, Risë Stevens, Set
Svanholm, Richard Tucker and John Brownlee.
Among designers whom Bing engaged in the course
of the years were Boris Aronson, Cecil Beaton,
Eugene Berman, Rolf Gérard, Desmond Heeley,
Oliver Messel, Ita Maximowna, Beni Montresor,
Günther Schneider-Siemssen, Franco Zeffirelli;
among stage directors were such theater and
Hollywood luminaries as Peter Brook, Tyrone

*The staircase of the Old Met
(top) and Sherry's Bar and
Restaurant on the Grand Tier
(above). At Sherry's, during the
Bing regime, the general
manager often played host at
dinner or during the
intermissions to artists and
members of the diplomatic
corps whom he entertained in
his box. Sherry's was a lively
place, a center for opera news,
rumor and gossip.*

21

Guthrie, Alfred Lunt, Joseph Mankiewicz, Cyril
Ritchard whose greatest success was Offenbach's
Perichole, and Margaret Webster, actress and
director of Shakespearean productions. George
Balanchine was persuaded to direct Stravinsky's
Rake's Progress. The team of Nathaniel Merrill and
Robert O'Hearn did eight productions.
In all, during the Bing time, there were eighty-seven
new productions though few contemporary works,
such as Menotti's *Last Savage*, Barber's *Vanessa* and
Antony and Cleopatra and Marvin David Levy's
Mourning Becomes Electra. He concentrated on
conductors: Solti, Karajan, Bernstein, Mitropoulos,
Stokowski, Monteux, Ansermet, Prêtre, Böhm,
Kempe, Rudolf; he brought back Fausto Cleva who
was to remain at the Met until he died. He gave
young conductors their big chance: Mehta,
Schippers, Maazel, Abbado, Keene. In 1971, during
the Met June Festival, he introduced a twenty-
seven-year-old conductor in *Tosca:* James Levine.
Only two years later Levine was appointed principal
conductor. In 1976 he became music director.
Rudolf Bing will also be remembered for the fact that
he broke the color bar, first in the chorus and ballet,
then by engaging a major singer, Marian Anderson
for Ulrica in *Ballo in Maschera*. That debut on
January 7, 1955, opened the doors of the
Metropolitan to a line of black artists, among them
Leontyne Price, Martina Arroyo, Grace Bumbry,
Shirley Verrett. Bing skimmed the cream of the
international market in singers. He brought to the
Met such sopranos and mezzos as Callas, Tebaldi,
Nilsson, Sutherland, Rysanek, Freni, Schwarzkopf,
Scotto, Caballé, Crespin, Söderström, Zylis-Gara,
Cossotto, Ludwig, Simionato. Nilsson's first
appearance as Isolde in 1959 created a sensation as
did Elisabeth Schwarzkopf's Marschallin in 1964. The
imported male list was impressive: Bergonzi, Corelli,
Del Monaco, Gedda, Valletti, Bacquier, Gobbi,
Sereni, Geraint Evans, Corena, Hotter, Ghiaurov,
Ruggero Raimondi, Talvela. Both Domingo and
Pavarotti began their Metropolitan Opera careers in
1968. Bing also brought Vickers from Canada as well
as Quilico. American artists on his roster included
Marilyn Horne, who joined the Met in 1970, and

Arturo Toscanini

Tullio Serafin

Bruno Walter

Sherrill Milnes, only twenty-nine when he began his long Met association in December 1965; also Blegen, Lear, Moffo, Farrell, Von Stade, Dunn, Elias, McCracken, Thomas, MacNeil, Stewart, Gramm, London, Tozzi, Macurdy, Morris, Plishka. With the move to Lincoln Center came a new era. The Metropolitan finally had a home with unrivalled stage facilities and acoustics, dominating Lincoln Center. *Newsweek* wrote: "The new Met, designed by architect Wallace K. Harrison, rules Lincoln Center like a queen, flanked by her courtiers, Philharmonic Hall and the New York State Theater." Opening night, September 16, 1966, was, despite the threat of an orchestra strike during final rehearsals and the breakdown of the giant turntable, a glittering, news-making occasion, attracting worldwide attention. The opera commissioned for the occasion was Barber's *Antony and Cleopatra*, with Leontyne Price—to whom Geraldine Farrar sent a laurel wreath—and Justino Díaz in the title roles. Thomas Schippers conducted. The great stage spectacle was designed and directed by Zeffirelli. *Antony and Cleopatra*—the score crushed under a weight of scenic effects—was not a great success. But a few weeks later, there was another elaborate production, Strauss' *Frau ohne Schatten*, with Leonie Rysanek, Christa Ludwig, James King and Walter Berry, and Karl Böhm conducting, which was a triumph. By this time everything on stage was in working order—sets advanced and retreated, rose into the air and descended into the earth. There was magic in the performance and the O'Hearn-Merrill production.

Another five seasons and Rudolf Bing announced his retirement. At a Farewell Gala on April 22, 1972, over fifty singers appeared to do him honor.

The next general manager, Goeran Gentele, was a modern man, who had been actor, director, and producer in films, theater and music. He had won a considerable reputation as head of the Royal Swedish Opera in Stockholm when the offer came from the Metropolitan. Much had been expected of him but he was officially general manager of the Metropolitan only eighteen days when, in July 1972, he was killed, while on vacation in Sardinia, in an automobile crash.

The Japanese white bridal satin souvenir program commemorating opening night at the new Met, September 16, 1966.

23

Rudolf Bing with Marc Chagall at the unveiling of the Chagall murals.

When the tragedy occurred Schuyler G. Chapin, whom Gentele had appointed as his assistant, became acting general manager. Chapin, who had had wide experience in concert management, recording and television and who had for some years been in charge of programming at Lincoln Center, set out to carry on Gentele's planned projects. There was the opening night *Carmen*, with Marilyn Horne in the title role, James McCracken as Don José and Leonard Bernstein conducting; with evocative sets by Czech designer Josef Svoboda; "a masterpiece of taste, wit, theatrical imagination," wrote *Time*. There was the first staged New York performance of Berlioz' *Les Troyens* and the American premiere of Britten's *Death in Venice*. There were the "Look-ins," to give young audiences an introduction to opera, with Danny Kaye in charge. There was the "Mini-Met" experiment at Lincoln Center's Forum, designed as a "second stage" to complement the main works at the opera house: Virgil Thomson's *Four Saints in Three Acts* and Purcell's *Dido and Aeneas* were featured. Gentele had appointed Rafael Kubelik music director but he remained only briefly. He was later succeeded by James Levine, then principal conductor. Meanwhile Chapin had strengthened the production end of the house by bringing stage director John Dexter from London for Verdi's *Vespri Siciliani*. It marked the first collaboration of Dexter and Levine. He also introduced Beverly Sills in Rossini's *Siege of Corinth*, its first performance at the Met, a production conducted by Thomas Schippers, staged by Sandro Sequi, with sets and costumes by Nicola Benois. That was April 7, 1975. At the end of May Chapin shepherded the company on a visit to Japan. When he returned his association with the Metropolitan was over. Chapin later became Dean of the School of the Arts of Columbia University. From 1975–76 to 1980–81 a triumvirate guided the Metropolitan. It consisted of Anthony A. Bliss as executive director—a title eventually changed to general manager—with James Levine first as principal conductor, then as music director, and John Dexter as director of production. In 1981 Dexter, wishing to be free of daily duties, became production adviser. The choice of Bliss as general manager was a natural one. He had been associated with the Metropolitan for more than half its history; opera is in his blood. Like his late father, Cornelius N. Bliss, he served both as board member and president of the Metropolitan Opera for many years. President of the board is Frank E. Taplin, a skilled musician, among other accomplishments; board chairman is William Rockefeller.

The great traditions remain but there are successful experiments as well as popular successes. Among offerings of special interest have been the complete Berg *Lulu* and Weill's *Mahagonny*, the Britten *Billy Budd* and the Poulenc *Dialogues of the Carmelites*, and the Satie-Poulenc-Ravel evening called *Parade*, dazzlingly directed and designed by John Dexter and David Hockney also later responsible for the Stravinsky Centenary evening of *Le Sacre du Printemps*, *Le Rossignol* and *Oedipus Rex*. A fresh approach to the classics has been shown in the complete *Don Carlo* and in the performance of Rossini's *Italiana in Algeri* in the new critical edition of the Rossini Foundation.

There was the first woman conductor at the Metropolitan, Sarah Caldwell in the pit for *Traviata* with Beverly Sills. There was a production of *Tannhäuser* which became an unprecedented hit. There was a constant healthy infusion of young singers but there were always the great artists, the favorites whose names spell box-office, in special revivals as well as standard repertoire: Joan Sutherland and Birgit Nilsson, Renata Scotto and Leonie Rysanek, Leontyne Price and Marilyn Horne, Placido Domingo, Luciano Pavarotti and Sherrill Milnes among them.

The Metropolitan is approaching its second century. First built for the pleasure of a group of millionaires, it now brings pleasure to the millions. It not only presents great performances at home but it carries them on tour to the entire country. Its Saturday afternoon operas have been broadcast since 1940; its telecasts are seen all over the world. *The New York Times* has stated: "Opera at the Metropolitan's best means the best there is anywhere."

Leontyne Price has the last words. "I love the Metropolitan Opera. For me, it's total Shangri-La."

The soaring, glass-panelled façade of the Metropolitan Opera House (overleaf) is a focal point for the countless visitors to Lincoln Center. It is a fairy-tale spectacle at night before a performance begins, when the house is lit, glowing with warmth and light. Lucky ones, tickets in hand, enter.

Anthony Bliss during a filming of the general manager's greeting to a telecast audience.

25

Exploring the Met

The Metropolitan Opera House is very much the *"grand dame"* of Lincoln Center. It moved into its new home (only the second in its history) September 16, 1966, bearing a tradition of memorable performances and internationally famous singers dating back to 1883. Lincoln Center awarded it a place of honor, rear and center, facing the impressive travertine plaza which has been likened to the Piazza San Marco of Venice. The largest of the Lincoln Center buildings, it was also the most expensive. However, unlike its neighboring constituents—Avery Fisher Hall, the New York State Theater and the Vivian Beaumont Theater, all of which eventually had to undergo radical renovations—the Metropolitan has remained virtually untouched. Its excellent acoustics were right from the start. The distinguished architect Wallace K. Harrison had said, quite simply, of his work: "It was built as a frame for the great operas of the world." The acoustical consultants, Vilhelm L. Jordan of Copenhagen and Cyril M. Harris of New York, were experts. Still, the first practical test was awaited with trepidation. It was a matinée for students; the opera was *La Fanciulla del West*. Harris nervously stationed himself high up in the Family Circle. After the famous poker game he reported: "I could hear every card go down. I knew then we really had a winner." On opening night the miracle of the acoustics was confirmed. "With the first note of the national anthem a $49 million sigh of relief went up." The facade of the Metropolitan Opera House is a place of pilgrimage for tourists with their cameras and a spectacle of which even New Yorkers never seem to tire. Its five great arches were designed so that passers-by can look through the glass panels into the illuminated house itself, can see the red-carpeted double staircase and the opulence of the gold-leaf ceiling, the glittering chandeliers and the radiant colors of the two huge Chagall paintings. And from within operagoers can watch the changing pageant on the plaza, one of New York's happiest and most colorful sights.

On entering the opera house from the plaza one goes through revolving doors into a long handsome lobby

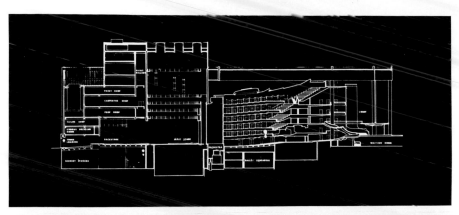

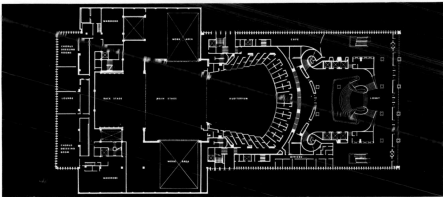

Architect Wallace Harrison's cross-sectional drawing (top) for the front and backstage areas of the opera house. The final floor plan (above) for the main level of the opera house.

A photograph taken from the fifth floor (overleaf) shows the central starburst chandelier crowning the pattern made by the sweep of the twin curves of the grand staircase. The ceiling is gold leaf. The carpets throughout are traditional "opera house red."

29

Its chandeliers are one of the Met's glories. The main chandelier (top) measures seventeen feet in diameter. The twelve satellite clusters are on a level with the Grand Tier and, when the house lights are dimmed and the performance about to begin, they ascend to the ceiling, often to the applause of newcomers to the house. Cleaning the chandeliers (above) is one of the Met's major housekeeping duties. They are lowered yearly, doused with ammonia water and polished with chamois, ready to shine on another season.

on the walls of which are marble plaques inscribed in gold with the names of Lincoln Center patrons. To the north, around a bend, is the main box office and beyond is a busy and attractive gift shop. Ushers wait behind central ornamental gates which are opened a half hour before curtain time to admit ticket-holders. Steps lead down to the orchestra lobby and to the auditorium itself. Before descending there is, on either side, the grand staircase which rises, in twin curves, to the Grand Tier. On gala nights the audience lines the steps to watch celebrities arrive or to cheer the appearance of a famous singer. On the top of the grand staircase is Lehmbruck's sculpture, *Kneeling Woman*, a gift of the German government. Among other art treasures in the house are three bronze figures by Aristide Maillol.

On both sides of the orchestra lobby are elevators, also fountains of marble given in memory of Ezio Pinza. On the south side stairs lead down to a lower lounge where during performances press staff and critics gather in a room lined with red banquettes. Beyond is the 144-seat List Hall used both for choral rehearsals and as the studio for the live intermission features of the Texaco Saturday afternoon broadcasts which have created and nourished over the years nation-wide audiences in this country and Canada.

The auditorium combines warmth and splendor, comfortable seats, 3,790 of them, and splendid sight lines. Suspended from its dome is a crystal chandelier, seventeen feet in diameter, and eight other starbursts of various sizes. Lower down are twelve satellite clusters. When house lights are dimmed and a performance is to begin, they slowly ascend to the ceiling, a very pretty sight. These magnificent chandeliers, some decorated with massive pieces of crystal and scores of crystal pearls, were the gift of the Austrian government.

Except for the ivory facings of the boxes everything in the house is red and gold. The fifty-four foot-high curtain is of gold damask. The seats are covered with red velour. Wood, called "sound's best friend," is used wherever possible, including the wall around the orchestra floor all of which came from a single

Many art treasures adorn the opera house. Among them are three bronze figures by the French sculptor, Aristide Maillol. Of the two shown here, Kneeling Woman-Monument to Debussy *(above) can be seen on the promenade of the Dress Circle and* Summer *(left) on the Grand Tier.*

33

The popular Gift Shop (top), located in the lobby near the box office. There one can buy records of opera and operatic vocal recitals, librettos, scores, books about music and musicians. There you can also find special gifts offered through the Metropolitan Opera Guild's Met-by-Mail catalogue, including opera glasses and jewelry, posters and postcards, evening bags and Metropolitan-imprinted umbrellas, music boxes, and the annual Guild calendar and Season book.

Founders Hall (above), which you will find on the concourse level. It is lined with portraits and busts of the opera's immortals, as well as paintings of the singers in their famous roles.

Congolese rosewood tree. When the trunk was cut
and acoustically treated veneers manufactured from
its sections, it yielded a material closely resembling
the moiré silk which had been architect Harrison's
inspiration.

The carefully planned orchestra pit can be moved up
or down according to the needs of the opera. It can
be raised for a small Mozart opera or lowered for the
large-size orchestra demanded by Wagner. The
conductor's podium is also adjustable to suit the
preferences or heights of the various maestri. The
hooded subsurface area for the prompter's box,
center-stage just behind the footlights, contains tiny
closed circuit TV screens focused on the conductor, a
phone for talking to the stage manager, a music rack
and a chair. Here the prompter (there is a staff of
three) sits, giving stage directions and vocal cues.
For the new or nervous artist he is as supportive as a
family doctor.

From the orchestra lobby one can go down, by
elevator or stairs, to the underground concourse
level where the public arrives if coming by subway,
taxi or private car. Inside the central entrance is
Founders Hall, its corridors lined with portraits and
busts of the Met's immortals. Dozens of singers, past
and present, are shown, many painted in the
costumes of their famous roles. The portraits, though
not great works of art, are richly evocative of
historic performances. To name a few: there are
Amelita Galli-Curci as Rosina, Lotte Lehmann as the
Marschallin, Maria Jeritza as Octavian, Louise
Homer—the contralto was an aunt of composer
Samuel Barber—as Orpheus. Chic Lily Pons is seen
in fur-trimmed blue velvet with a live bird perched
on a finger. On display also are Giovanni Martinelli
as Otello, Lauritz Melchior as Tristan (the Isolde,
Kirsten Flagstad, is shown in a concert gown),
Feodor Chaliapin as the Czar Boris, Giuseppe De
Luca as Rigoletto, Ezio Pinza as Don Giovanni,
Leonard Warren as Simon Boccanegra, Richard
Tucker as Andrea Chénier and Enrico Caruso in the
last role he ever sang, Eléazar in *La Juive*. There
are also busts, including Marian Anderson, Toscanini
and Bruno Walter, Caruso, Bjoerling and Scotti,
Giulio Gatti-Casazza and Sir Rudolf Bing, not to

*From Founders Hall, portraits
of (top) Maria Jeritza as
Octavian in* Der Rosenkavalier
*and (below) Leo Slezak as
Otello.*

On the landing of the Parterre Box level, an attention-drawing display is the changing exhibition of costumes worn by Metropolitan Opera singers in roles associated with them. In the vitrines (top) are medieval gowns which Kirsten Flagstad wore as Isolde and the richly ornamented crown and coronation robe (above) of George London as the Czar Boris Godunov.

mention Mozart, Beethoven and the Gemito bronze of Verdi. History on these walls goes back to Marcella Sembrich, who sang Lucia the second night of the Metropolitan's first season, October 24, 1883. Returning to the orchestra lobby one can ascend, either from the far right or far left, to the Parterre Box level. There are twenty-nine boxes, each with a mirrored anteroom. The plush walls and carpets are garnet red. One of the boxes is permanently reserved for the general manager. A private passageway leads from the corridor to his office suite. Among the attractions of the Parterre Box level are the two glass showcases, a changing exhibition of historic costumes worn by great singers.

From the grand staircase one can walk to the Grand Tier level where one finds the great glory of the opera house, the two thirty-by-thirty-six foot paintings of Chagall. The mural on the north side, its color harmonies dominated by yellow, is called "The Sources of Music"; the one on the south, with rich red as the prevailing color, is entitled "The Triumph of Music." Both are reproduced in this book. The Grand Tier also provides a restaurant for pre-performance dining and entr'acte snacks and a large serpentine bar, a popular intermission rendezvous. On pleasant nights doors lead to an outdoor terrace, overlooking the plaza below. On the outer edge of the portico there are two abstract granite sculptures by the Japanese artist Masayuki Nagare. They are enlargements in the form of the classic *bachi*, of the carved tools used to pluck the samisen, a stringed guitar-like instrument traditionally played by geishas to accompany their singing.

Also on the Grand Tier is the Eleanor Belmont Room, named for Mrs. Eleanor Belmont, the great lady who literally saved the Metropolitan in 1933 and who founded the Metropolitan Opera Guild for whose members this room is reserved. It is used at times for special events. There is a handsome portrait of Mrs. Belmont on the wall, also a framed collection of composers' autographs and letters. On the console are the hands of Lucrezia Bori, modelled in bronze; this charming soprano was the only active artist ever to become a member of the board of directors of the

A night at the Met often starts on the Chagall-ornamented Grand Tier (above) with a dinner at the restaurant. Views of the surrounding plaza can be seen by diners. During intermissions many stop for a drink at the nearby serpentine bar (left).

The Sources of Music
The central double-headed
figure holding a lyre is both
King David and Orpheus,
symbolizing the union of East
and West in music. The floating
horizontal figure is the "Angel
Mozart," enclosing characters
from The Magic Flute. *The pair*
of lovers, below and to the right,
is Chagall's "Homage to Verdi."
The "Tree of Life" hovers above
the Manhattan skyline.

The Triumph of Music
The great winged figure with trumpet is "The Musician." At the bottom of the right border of the mural is a blue tree. To the right of the blue tree is a tiny figure balancing herself with a parasol. Chagall identifies her as his wife. He himself is the seated figure on the left. The painter pays homage to American, French and Russian music through jazz, opera and folk references.

Metropolitan. In one corner is another of the Met's treasures, a mask in colored wax of Anna Pavlova, done from life by Malvina Hofmann. Pavlova was a member of the Metropolitan Ballet for two seasons. She made an extraordinary debut in *Coppélia*, partnered by Milhail Mordkin, on February 28, 1910, following a performance of the opera *Werther*.

Above the Grand Tier comes the Dress Circle. The board room, reserved for patrons in the evening, is located on this level as is the Metropolitan Opera Club, founded in 1894. Club members were once known as the penguins because of the starched shirt fronts without which they never appeared at the opera. By now top hats have disappeared as have white ties except perhaps on still fashionable Monday nights but members of varied professional and business backgrounds remain united in one basic thing—their shared passion for opera.

Finally one reaches the Family Circle and Balcony where another friendly bar awaits. Side seats on the Family Circle level are utilized for single rows of chairs and illuminated score-desks, for students to follow a score during a performance. In the theater the top of the house is known as "the peanut gallery." In Italian opera houses it is named the *"piccionaia"*—the pigeons' loft. Call it what you will, it is the place where many an opera fan was initiated into the world of grand opera, where—hearing the operas of Mozart, Verdi and Puccini, of Beethoven, Strauss and Wagner—they learned what makes grand opera grand. As Francis Robinson wrote: "There is always somebody hearing *La Bohème* for the first time."

In the Belmont Room on the Grand Tier, one of the three large frames containing an interesting array of autographs and letters of composers ranging from Bach to Berg.

Members of the Metropolitan Opera Guild have access to the Eleanor Belmont Room (above) on the Grand Tier for a drink and visit with friends during the intermission of a Met performance.

A typical night at the Metropolitan (overleaf). The opera is about to start. The audience waits, suddenly still.

Cross-section of the backstage area of the Met (second overleaf) with the audience in place, the sets of La Gioconda on all four stages, glimpses into the dressing rooms, rehearsal rooms, storage and loading areas and the various construction and maintenance shops. (Illustration by Donald A. Mackay)

Donald A. Finkel

A construction (opposite) is translated from small scale designs and blueprints into stage-size sets for Il Barbière di Siviglia.

An outstanding traditional scenic design (overleaf): Act II of Rossini's Assedio di Corinto, the Turkish Emperor's tent, realistic flats painted in glowing reds, blues and golds. The stage designer was Nicola Benois.

Act II of La Bohème (second overleaf), the Latin Quarter, Paris, on Christmas Eve in the spectacular set of "romantic realist" Franco Zeffirelli.

Set models (above), designed by Robin Wagner for the 1982 production of Il Barbiere di Siviglia.

Backstage World

Newsweek wrote of the new Met in 1966: "It triumphs as a container for a vast and supermodern theatrical technology." Francis Robinson called it "a world of wonders." Yet few understand that the Metropolitan has two worlds, the stage world and the backstage world, in which make-believe is made possible. For every new opera production there are endless technical preparations. The hard work and skills of hundreds of employees precede each glamorous opening night.

Set Design

The immensity of the backstage world is overwhelming. It is here that a production begins. The designer and director have a visual conception of how a production should look onstage. That vision must be translated into the reality of scenery, props, wigs, costumes, makeup and lighting on the Met stage.

Many designers are unfamiliar with the mechanics of the house and need the Met's resident scenic, costume and lighting designers to help them understand the possibilities and functions of the various shops as well as the stage itself. Resident designers often provide an intermediate stage of translation for visiting designers in the form of scale drawings, plans and details from tiny models, quick sketches or simply verbal ideas based on photographic research. It is not unusual for a designer to spend long hours researching for historical accuracy. The resident designers are responsible for the development of the production from inception to opening.

The shops begin their work on a production once the myriad details of scale, scenic and costume materials, numbers and casting for costumes, plan for hanging, shifting and lighting scenery, special effects, lighting and so on are agreed upon.

Carpentry

On entering the carpentry shop one is greeted by a wonderful smell of fresh lumber—piled up, cut up, built up. Sounds of hammers and saws fill the air. Ships, staircases, stone walls, ramps, towers, garret rooms, palaces and gambling dens, mountains and caves are all constructed by carpenters, frequently from doll-sized models. Wood, the primary material, takes numerous forms in the shop: sheets of plywood in different thicknesses and finishes, pressed composition board and dimensional lumber in all shapes. Special moldings and trimmings are created in the shop with lathes and shaping machines. Plastics formed under heat, fiberglass, foam, fabric, plexiglass and metal also are used in the construction of scenery. The sewing equipment for drops, ground cloths and scrims is housed here.

For lightness and ease of handling, much of the scenery consists of wooden frames which fold and are hinged or tied together. These frames are covered with fabric and eventually will be painted by scenic artists. It may take thirty or forty flat wings, attached and set in various shapes, to complete a single scene.

Other scenic elements are actually built: they contain the real detail of architecture and everyday objects, but even here illusion is important. Everyday materials are often too heavy for the stage. Foam and hollow constructions are used to suggest the reality of heavy objects, as in the huge *Otello* towers. Another consideration is the need for everything to break apart into small pieces for storage and transport. Everything is carefully labelled with the name of the opera, act and scene. It is all like a great jigsaw puzzle. Occasionally the set for an entire opera consists of one object. For *Billy Budd* it was an enormous replica of an eighteenth-century British man-of-war. The carpentry shop built a ship with three decks which operated on the stage lifts. As the opera proceeded, various levels were revealed by moving whole sides of the ship up and down.

Two highly skilled draftsmen from the carpentry shop (opposite) measure small models from which the huge pieces of a Metropolitan opera production will be constructed.

The building of the second scene of the second act of La Traviata *(overleaf) gives an idea of the scale of construction.*

A photograph (second overleaf) taken from behind the main stage during a technical rehearsal of Otello. *We see the great flight of steps leading down to the quay, and the enormous "stone" towers, which are constructed of molded fiberglass.*

Scenic Department

The curtain rises. The setting for the first act is revealed—a garret looking out on the rooftops of Paris (*La Bohème*), the Imperial City (*Turandot*), a Japanese house and garden (*Butterfly*), a ball in the palace of the Duke of Mantua (*Rigoletto*), the magical abode of Venus (*Tannhäuser*) and dozens of other absorbing and breath-taking sights.

The scenic department begins work on a new production by making full-scale paper patterns for difficult scenic pieces from which the carpenters can build. These designs are translated directly from the mechanical drawings or the designer's color sketches or models. A backdrop seventy feet high may have evolved from a drawing perhaps sixteen by twenty *inches*. Special materials and treatments are tested to achieve the unique and unusual effects of stone, wood, foliage, mirror or metal. Mundane materials like paper, sawdust, chopped foam, rags, glue and old rope are transformed into the most elegant or ancient-looking final product.

Soft scenery is sewn in the carpentry shop and sent to the scenic department to be painted. Many different kinds of fabrics are used; all are fireproofed. Groundcloths are made of a heavy cotton duck to withstand hard wear. Tacked out tight on the floor of the shop, a piece of plain duck becomes an inlaid marble floor, the deck of an ancient ship or the dirt courtyard of an inn. Opaque drops are made of duck, starched muslin is used for a translucent effect and a variety of scrims and gauzes for transparent or atmospheric effects.

Slides which may represent entire landscapes as in *Tannhäuser* or abstract patterns as in *Die Frau ohne Schatten* are painted or photographed by scenic artists. Props, chandeliers and even costumes often need painting and they receive careful attention along with the larger pieces of scenery. Tools vary from traditional brushes to stencils, rollers and graining devices made to suit a special scenic problem. Some tools, for instance, are used to "distress" props and costumes, to remove their brand-new fresh-from-the-shops look.

The scenic department has facilities to paint vertically or horizontally. A scenic artist (opposite) paints with comfort and facility on the floor. Brushes and drawing materials mounted on bamboo or metal poles allow the artist to work upright, providing a more expansive view of his/her work, as well as a better sweeping motion.

A "still life" of the scenic department (overleaf). The huge cans of paint come in every color of the rainbow, every shade of every hue. Ninety-nine percent of the paint is water-based for safety and convenience in clean-up.

The paint bridge (opposite) with two huge electrically-operated frames that work up and down between floors. Canvas or other materials are tacked to the frames. Artists paint from stationary platforms while frames move as needed.

Brushes in every length, of every variety (above), hang on the walls of the scenic shop.

Electric Shop

The public applauds the scenery and costumes of a beautiful or evocative set, but is not always aware of the atmosphere and illusion created by lighting. Yet it is largely through lighting that a scene projects a feeling of joy or gloom or fear, a sense of dawn or dusk or midnight. It is lighting which, through all sorts of visual tricks, brings magic to the stage Special electric props—the arch of lights in *Mahagonny*, chandeliers, torches, lamps, electrically-driven mechanical effects—are developed and built here. Electric equipment, from stage lights and machinery to sewing machines, is supplied and maintained here.

The electric shop not only houses electrical props but files for color media, projectors and special effects. Fire, for example, is created with smoke, steam and projections. Lightning is made by using strobe lights or old-style flash bulbs. Moving clouds are created by placing a painted disc in front of a projector. Stars can be achieved in various ways, including an ingenious "star-drop," a black velour drop onto which hundreds of tiny lights are sewn.

The master light control room is located at the rear of the auditorium. The computer-driven lighting system can control up to 500 dimmers with no limit to the number of cues. An average performance uses most of the house's 300 lights positioned in the ceiling, on the four lighting bridges that hang high over the stage, in the proscenium and on the towers on either side of the stage. It is hard to remember that it was in a gas-lit house that the Metropolitan opened its doors in 1883.

Chandeliers and other lights made in the prop shop are wired in the electrical shop (opposite). This handsome chandelier was destined for La Traviata.

Prop Shop

The prop shop has the attraction of an antiques store or a flea market. It is, however, an orderly and efficient production center for everything from fountains, furniture, rocks and statues to pictures, curtains and draperies. Upholstery is also made here, usually out of canvas or linen, to be painted later by the scenic shop.

A prop can be anything: the silver rose Octavian brings to Sophie, the table knife with which Tosca stabs Scarpia, the flower Carmen tosses to Don José, the bottled Elixir of Love Dr. Dulcamara sells the guileless Nemorino, the Sphinx from *Antony and Cleopatra*, the Trojan Horse from *Les Troyens*, the falling snow in *La Bohème*, the huge roast served in the gluttony scene of *Mahagonny*. Props are made of everything from wood and clay to plastics and cardboard. Most important is that they be both sturdy and light. The shaggy-bark trees in *Jenufa* look solid and heavy. But, made of cardboard-covered fiberglass, they can easily be lifted. Fiberglass, butarine and polystyrene (thermal plaster sheets) have certainly liberated theater props. Molding techniques begin with sculpting the desired shapes in styrofoam, clay or wood. Statues are carved individually from styrofoam, then coated with plaster or aluminum foil, and often covered with fiberglass. The carousel horses for *Bartered Bride* were made this way. The enormous teapot from *L'Enfant et les Sortilèges* is ingeniously held together with a pin which two little boys operate from inside so that it can break apart as needed. Small props are frequently purchased and adapted to a specific need. The stage prop department maintains a large supply of stock items—walking sticks, umbrellas, eye glasses, trays, kettles, coffee pots, cups and saucers, goblets in a variety of periods and styles.

Props from Hansel and Gretel *(opposite) have been brought to the stage in a laundry basket awaiting their use: the wicked witch stretched out and a cut-out of the gingerbread figure into which she has been baked in the oven.*

A dramatic scene from Berlioz' Les Troyens *(overleaf). After Cassandra prophesies the fall of Troy the Trojans celebrate their victory over the Greeks, unaware that the wooden horse which the Greeks have left behind will prove to be the destruction of the city. Shown here is a large lion figure from* Les Troyens *made in the Met prop shop.*

Costumes and Wardrobe

Some operas require few costumes. Others like *Aida* with its triumphal march scene—require a hundred or more. Occasionally a director dictates what is needed. In the last *La Bohème* production, Franco Zeffirelli asked costume designer Peter J. Hall for close to three hundred costumes! He wanted a crowd of over one hundred and fifty, a chorus of eighty, thirty-five children, stage band of twelve—this plus cast. Among the costumes were women's dresses, demure in their period charm, with billowing underskirts which were carefully sewn to the hand-made corsets. At the Met a costume is not to be trifled with.

The second floor of the Metropolitan is where all the picturesque costumes for operas of every time and every kind are made, not only for solo artists but for chorus, ballet, supers and "covers."

Costume designer, set designer and director work closely together to establish the period and general appearance of a new production. The sketches from the costume designer can be anything from pen-and-ink sketches to fully painted portraits. The resident costume designer must frequently provide intermediate sketches and is generally responsible for the development of the costume from first sketch to the performance. In the resident costume designer's office are bolts and samples of material on shelves, costume sketches with fabric swatches attached piled on a table, loose-leaf binders containing detailed records of past productions: photostats of sketches, detailed notes. There is also a set of measurements for each artist, chorus and ballet member. Men work on the men's costumes and women on the women's. There are seamstresses and tailors who can take a basic shape in muslin and adapt it to the design on which they are working without going through the preliminaries of making a paper pattern and sample muslin. Every effort is made to minimize the weight of the costume without losing the desired effect. But the glittering stone-studded robe made for the Czar Boris in the Coronation Scene of *Boris Godunov* is so heavy it takes a strong artist like Martti Talvela to carry it. To this day it is remembered with awe that the

Peter J. Hall's costume drawings (opposite) for La Bohème (sets by Franco Zeffirelli) and colorful sketches for Un Ballo in Maschera (sets by Peter Wexler).

master himself, Chagall, hand-painted several of the costumes for *The Magic Flute*. Storeroom and drawers overflow with accessories and trimmings: ribbons and laces, buttons and beads and jewels. There are rows of boots and hats and there is material which can be turned into padded shapes for the fat bellies of *opera buffa* characters or into a hump for Rigoletto. And there are bolts and bolts of fabric. Natural materials are preferred to synthetics. Costumes must be made to last ten to fifteen years. Finished costumes hang in splendor on racks.

The wardrobe department is responsible for storage and maintenance of the costumes once they are completed. Each season the wardrobe department handles some 4,000 to 5,000 costumes used in current productions. Costumes for operas not in the present year's repertory are stored in the Met's warehouse until needed. The wardrobe department also will select and deliver to the costume shop any costume needing major alterations to accommodate new cast members. Members of the wardrobe staff function as dressers during a performance, placing the appropriate costumes in the artists' dressing rooms, assisting with difficult costume changes, and providing emergency on-the-spot repairs. Some operas have special wardrobe requirements: *Lulu*, for instance, has seven very fast onstage costume changes for which a dresser must be present just out of sight of the audience. In *Manon Lescaut* a dresser must be onstage, in costume herself, to assist Manon in a costume change which is part of the stage action.

Sketches by British designer Deirdre Clancy for her first Met opera, Così fan Tutte: Dorabella (opposite) and Guglielmo (above) in his Albanian disguise.

Wigs

A costume, of course, needs a wig or a special hair style to complete it and so it is natural that the Met wig department should adjoin the costume shop. Wigs for all the singers, plus chorus and ballet members, are styled and often made by the wig department always after consultation with the costume designer. Wigs are made both from natural hair, often Oriental, and from synthetic hair. Processed human hair is bought from hair brokers in New York, who obtain it at auctions from worldwide sources. White wigs, however, come from the yak, a long-haired Tibetan ox. Gray hair is the hardest natural hair to find. To look natural, a wig is made with many colors of hair. For Melisande's floor-length wig seven different shades were intermingled "to give it life." The wig of Birgit Nilsson in *Salome* was made of dark hair mixed with green-black cock feathers.

Before making a wig the measurements of the artist's head are taken. A block is adjusted to these measurements and covered with the foundation—a heavy net with fine tulle near the hairline and a stiff material at the base of the neck. Hairs are woven through the net by hand with a fine hook and knotted, singly in the front, and four at a time in the back. Each wig requires about thirty-five hours of hand work, and about four to five ounces of hair.

Two hours before the start of every performance a member of the wig staff is backstage to assist the artists in putting on their wigs or to help dress the hair of principal artists not wearing wigs. Every morning all wigs used the night before are cleaned. Wigs, carefully labelled, are stored in specially constructed boxes. For a popular opera such as *Butterfly* there may be as many as a dozen or more boxes labelled with the names of the artists who have sung the title role, from Tebaldi and Kirsten and Price to Lorengar, Zylis-Gara and Scotto.

Occasionally the costume designer will actually supply sketches of the wigs for the artists to wear as Peter J. Hall did for Un Ballo in Maschera *(above).*

Makeup

The makeup concept is determined by the costume designer and director with the makeup artist. Sometimes the costume designer will actually sketch out a plan for the makeup if the production is highly stylized, as is the Met production of *Aida*. But more frequently the makeup artist will sketch his own makeup design from the costume design. Special pieces such as beards and mustaches, bald spots and scars, are also prepared, styled and maintained here in the makeup department which is involved with anything from changing noses to orientalizing eyes to scarring faces. For special character makeup latex pieces are molded from casts of an artist's face. For the makeup man a vital concern is to see that the structure of the face carries to the farthest reaches of the house. If the basic structure is not there, it must be constructed.

With costume and wig assembled, the night of the performance arrives. Makeup completes the singer's transformation. The staff is available before each performance to assist in the application of the makeup, a process which can take anywhere from fifteen minutes to an hour, depending on the complexity of the character or image the artist is to assume. The staff is also on hand during performances to do touch-ups, reglue eyelashes, wipe down or renew makeup and so forth. Most important for the artist is that he or she "look good."

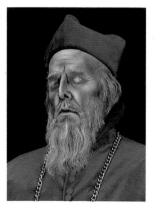

Through artful makeup, young James Morris attains blind old age (above); the basso as the Grand Inquisitor in Verdi's Don Carlo.

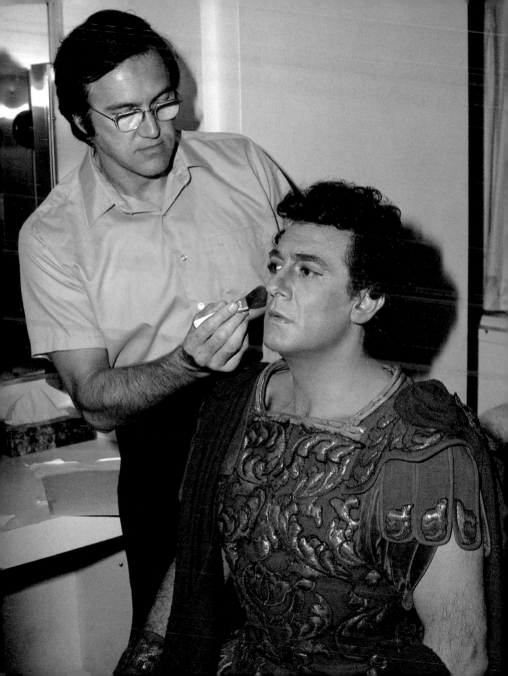

Storage and Rehearsal Rooms

The opera house extends three floors underground, so far down that, during construction, water was reached. The first floor below, known as A level, contains the conductor's room, musicians' lounge and locker rooms. There are also locker rooms and lounges for electricians, carpenters, prop men. B level is used for scenery, prop and electric storage. The music library is also housed on B level. In addition to the great storage area to the rear of the building, C level contains the main rehearsal stage, orchestra and ballet rehearsal rooms, and offices. Here all the preparation for an opera performance takes place until chorus and orchestra, cast and—when needed—dancers move upstairs for final rehearsals onstage. The rehearsal rooms are nearly two stories high, each equipped with *barres* and mirrors. The ballet room has a special resilient maple flooring. It is used during the season by the Metropolitan Opera Ballet and in summer by guest companies. The main rehearsal room is soundproof; its proximity to the storage area makes it convenient to move in set pieces to work with. The orchestra room was treated for sound and approximates the acoustical properties of the auditorium itself. The room is also used for the *Sitzprobe*, a German term which identifies a seated rehearsal with orchestra, chorus and principals. Both stage and orchestra rooms are hung with delightful backdrops made by Raoul Dufy for Anouilh's *Ring Around the Moon*. The play was produced by Gilbert Miller who, when it closed, gave the valuable sets to the Met. A third hangs on the walls of what used to be the "Top of the Met" restaurant. The Dufy mural, hiding acoustical materials in the orchestra rehearsal room, is an appropriate scene: the Avenue de l'Opéra with the Paris Opera in the background.

The Metropolitan has a vast storage area (above and opposite), three clear stories high, which occupies the underground space to the rear of the building. An enormous elevator leads from here to the stage. The space can accommodate sets for an average of six complete productions. The rest is stored in warehouses to be brought out when needed.

Coaching and Directing

There is no end to the care and training of an opera singer. The voice is only the beginning. Then there are languages and diction to be studied, roles to be memorized, stage presence to be acquired and, finally, the art of acting while singing to be learned. Young singers arrive at the Met in various ways. To be a finalist in the Metropolitan Opera National Council annual auditions sometimes leads to the coveted contract—as was the case with such artists as Arroyo, Bumbry, Cruz-Romo, Stratas, Verrett, Díaz and Milnes. But often singers are engaged after training and performing abroad, or with America's increasingly good regional opera companies. Music director James Levine has called the Metropolitan "a home for American singers," but basically it is the voice, not its place of origin, which governs the decision.

Once at the Met, artists have at their disposal training of any kind from vocal and diction coaches to stage directors. They are helped to become proficient in everything from posture and gesture to movement and makeup. And, if they are men, they have an additional skill to master: they must be taught to fence with agility and style. Duel scenes, as pictured in old opera books, would be laughed off the stage today. Now male singers learn footwork, timing and basic theatrics, and always use swords appropriate to the opera's period. Battle scenes must be realistic, historic and, above all, rhythmic—the beats of the blades in tempo with the music. Three weapons in use at the Met should not be confused: the foil, the épée and the sabre. A Met fencing master said: "They are as different as tennis, squash and badminton."

Preliminary rehearsals are held in rehearsal rooms on C level, or on the second floor of the opera house for individual or small group coaching. Artists study and rehearse their roles with great care and work out their interpretations with the authoritative stage directors who create new productions at the Met. The days are long since gone when opera singers needed for their careers only a collection of stock melodramatic gestures—the outstretched arm, the downcast head, the bended knee, the wiggled hip,

John Dexter (opposite) has been responsible for directing some of the most exciting and innovative Met productions since making his debut with I Vespri Siciliani. The scope of his talent has been revealed in operas ranging from Dialogues of the Carmelites to Lulu, Billy Budd and the brilliant Parade, a Satie-Poulenc-Ravel triple bill. Here he is at an early rehearsal of Ravel's Enfant et les Sortilèges. The rehearsal version of these large children's alphabet blocks were actually colored by the performing children under the direction of designer David Hockney.

En garde! Fencing lessons (overleaf) are part of every male singer's training. One must be coached to learn how to coordinate hand and footwork for the duels and battles which are part and parcel of grand opera.

the clutched brow—to express exultation or despair, fealty or vengeance, allure or abandonment. The Metropolitan had for a number of years as director of productions the brilliant British-born John Dexter. In his present capacity as production adviser, Dexter still works closely with James Levine, advising on all stage and production aspects of the theater, as well as directing certain new productions each season and supervising revivals of productions he originally created.

Assistant stage directors are present at every rehearsal. They are there to record all changes requested by the director and must then see that the requests are actually carried out. These requests could include anything from changes in chorus entrances and exits to substitutions or additions to the props, or adjustments to costumes. The assistant director's notes become the definitive written word on the staging of a production. They are stored away and consulted for any future revival. The stage director is usually not available for revival productions, so the assistant director functions alone to recreate the original staging. The importance of those staging notes cannot be overstated.

A working rehearsal on the stage of the Metropolitan (opposite). John Dexter is seen coaching the cast in Mozart's Entführung aus dem Serail. Designs by Jocelyn Herbert were influenced by Turkish and Persian miniatures. Dexter adjusts the cloak of Belmonte, the noble hero (above). He has come to rescue his beloved Constanze, held captive in the house of the Pasha Selim.

James Levine, principal conductor (opposite), working in the orchestra rehearsal room on C level. The lively Dufy mural visible behind Maestro Levine shows the Paris Opera in the background.

The Met orchestra (overleaf) rehearsing for Carmen *under the baton of Leonard Bernstein (1972).*

Met musicians in the orchestra pit (above) during a performance.

Orchestra, Chorus and Ballet

Opera News has written: "The soul of the Metropolitan Opera House is the orchestra pit." The Metropolitan Opera Orchestra is rightly considered one of the best in the world. It is also one of the most highly paid since its members must be top musicians, combining exceptional professional skills, musical knowledge and practical experience with sheer stamina. They must be able to play everything from Rossini to Verdi and Puccini, from Gounod to Massenet and Meyerbeer, from Moussorgsky and Wagner to Janáček and Poulenc, from Britten to Berg. If a singer should by accident skip a line the orchestra must be as quick as the conductor to catch and cover the mistake.

For orchestra members the Metropolitan is a second home. Work begins three weeks before the season starts, five days a week, five and a half hours of rehearsal daily. The amount of time devoted to a new work depends on the opera itself. Fifty hours, including general rehearsal, were accorded to *Lulu*. A revival of *Siegfried* needed about thirty hours; a new production of a standard piece such as *La Traviata* about twenty-five hours.

Stamina is especially needed for the long nights when *Götterdämmerung*, for example, is played, or *Parsifal*, which lasts five hours, of which over four is playing time. Yet even the shortest work in the Met repertory, *Salome* is almost an hour and a half, about as long as the average symphony program. The full complement of one hundred musicians is used for operas such as *Elektra* or *Götterdämmerung*, where the number is augmented by an extra twelve onstage for the hunting scene. The opera with the smallest orchestra is *Ariadne auf Naxos*, thirty-seven. For Mozart—*Così fan Tutte* or *Le Nozze di Figaro*—the orchestra can vary from forty-eight to fifty-two.

In recent years the orchestra has had the chance to be appreciated on the stage at the Metropolitan. There James Levine has conducted it in a Wagner-Strauss concert with Birgit Nilsson, the Verdi Requiem, a concert with Pavarotti as soloist, a concert with Domingo and Troyanos, as well as one with Horne and Price.

With the orchestra, the Metropolitan Opera Chorus is responsible for the high day-to-day quality of performance. It consists of eighty musically trained men and women who are capable of singing in a variety of styles regularly in Italian, French and German, occasionally in Russian and English, often on very short notice. Choristers have to project and shape every phrase they sing with precision, always thinking about ensemble details, such as entrances, cutoffs and sixteenth-notes, not to mention staying in balance with each other and the orchestra. This ability to stay in balance with each other is one of the qualities looked for in a chorister's audition. Solo qualities and temperament are out of place. A chorister must think and act differently than a soloist. Basically what's needed is a voice of some size and clarity, used with intelligence. Since rehearsals are so costly, there simply is no time to repeat passages over and over.

In some cases, chorus parts are even longer than soloists. *Lohengrin*, for example, requires tenor choristers to sing more than the protagonist himself. Many opera choruses are as familiar as famous arias, from the Bridal Chorus of *Lohengrin* and the Anvil Chorus of *Trovatore* to the "Gloria all' Egitto" of *Aida* and the nostalgic "Va pensiero" of *Nabucco*. Great stamina is needed to combat the exhausting physical demands of the repertory system.

At the Met, there is also a Children's Chorus, featured in such operas as *Carmen*, *La Bohème* and *Hansel and Gretel*.

Chorus, orchestra, singers, all profit by the Met's library treasury, 4,000 vocal scores of eighty works and full sets of orchestra parts for sixty operas.

Chorus of Don Pasquale *(opposite), charmingly garbed by set and costume designer Desmond Heeley.*

The Metropolitan Opera Chorus in Die Meistersinger *(overleaf), picturesquely costumed in 16th-century Nuremberg style.*

Ballet is often a stepchild of the opera and it is only within recent years that the Met has brought it into the family. It is true that in the past the Metropolitan had made various efforts to elevate the status of its ballet, such as when, in the thirties, Edward Johnson engaged Balanchine as ballet master and when, during the Bing regime, Antony Tudor was brought in for a season as choreographer and when later, in the sixties, Dame Alicia Markova was appointed resident director. But for a considerable time ballet was not the Met's strongest feature and it is only in recent years that the importance of ballet has been recognized. The quality of the ballet is now such that, when featured in operas like *Traviata* or *Tannhäuser* or *La Gioconda*, it is recognized as an integral and visually absorbing part of the performance.

The Metropolitan Opera Ballet consists of twenty-three dancers of which ten are men; extras are added when needed. They are trained in every form of dance, from the Balanchine-devised Polonaise in *Boris Godunov* and the gypsy dances choreographed by Alvin Ailey for *Carmen* to the decadently beautiful beach dances designed by Frederick Ashton for *Death in Venice* or the spectacular bull-jumping which Todd Bolender created for *The Trojans*. The company was given even higher status when it danced the ballet *Parade*, the first part of the Met's French triple bill of Satie, Poulenc, and Ravel and *Le Sacre du Printemps* in the Stravinsky evening.

An offshoot of the company is the Metropolitan Opera Ballet Ensemble, which gives lecture demonstrations in the public schools and, as part of the Met's Education project conceived by John Dexter, does children's productions such as *The Story of Babar* and *Peter and the Wolf*. The ballet-story of the baby elephant Babar was so successful that it was shown at the White House at the annual party given by the President for children of the diplomatic corps.

Right: Two dancers warming up for the Traviata ballet. In the background, stagehands are changing the set.

Following two pages: Smetana's Bartered Bride; the Met settings for the Czech opera were by Svoboda, the costumes by Jan Skalicky. In this scene the circus comes to the village. The dancing couple featured is really a single dancer ingeniously manipulating a dummy.

The Stage

At the Met all the world's a stage, and the Metropolitan has the biggest and best equipped stage in the world. Its vast area contains the 101-by-80-foot main stage—revealed to the audience when the golden curtain opens—backed by a rear stage and flanked by two side stages. In all, the space is six times larger than the stage area of the old house. Traditional waits between scenes need no longer exist. Each of the side stages and the rear stage can contain a complete set, ready to be rolled into position. This is done with "stage wagons" or moving platforms on casters upon which a setting or a section of a setting can be mounted, up to thirty feet high, and wheeled onto the main platform. The stage at the back carries a huge turntable, used for the *The Bartered Bride* curtain calls, making the carousel revolve.

The main stage is in seven sections, any one of which can be raised or lowered hydraulically. It has fifty-two traps, for supernatural appearances and descents, and it has electrical outlets of every kind and for every purpose. The front three elevators have a floor underneath that can be pre-set and raised during a performance. In *Die Frau ohne Schatten* producer Nathaniel Merrill took full advantage of such special effects: the sets come forward and go back, rise into the air into the fly area or descend into the depths.

There are two cycloramas, white and blue; they can look calm or stormy depending on the cloud slides of the electrical department. In use, the cyclorama surrounds the stage from the floor to a height of 108 feet.

Behind the stage are the principal artists' dressing rooms. Each has a piano, dressing table, full-length triple mirror, bathroom with shower, telephone and loudspeaker from the stage. These rooms are the only ones, except for the general manager's office, where there are windows which open. Costumes are placed in the rooms before the performance. Names of the artists are put on the doors.

The empty stage (above), looking through the proscenium arch to the warm red and gold of the auditorium. The house lights are up, the tiers of seats are visible. The proscenium towers seen on either side of the stage opening allow for adjustment in the width of the stage opening.

Overleaf

1. Stage manager's console, which includes, among other things, switches for cue lights in all stage locations, warning signal buttons for dressing rooms, studios and offices; closed-circuit TV monitors for cameras on stage and conductor and controls for the house chimes.

2. Various types of stage lights on floor stands stored offstage.

3. Mainstage as seen from stage left wagon. The proscenium is to the left, beyond the ladder.

4. The fly system, 110 feet above the stage floor. There are 103 battens or "pipes" to fly curtains, scenery, backdrops, scrims. Miraculous entrances can be made from the fly system.

5. The lighting booth at rear of auditorium. The large yellow panels are actually a backup system for the main computer-driven Strand Century "Light Palette" system, the consoles of which you can see to the right. The "Light Palette" will automatically run up to six cues simultaneously in timed fades from 0–999 seconds. Since the memory can be reloaded in seven seconds, there is no real limitation on the number of lighting cues in a production.

6. View of the main stage floor, with its elevators and trap doors, from one of the galleries high above the stage floor.

7. The first of four light bridges which stretch across the stage carrying a variety of lighting instruments. The bridge carries the black "teaser" curtain which adjusts the vertical dimension of the proscenium opening.

8. One of the two proscenium towers which carries lighting equipment and permits variation in the width of the stage opening. Also visible is the TV monitor for the camera on the conductor; performers can watch the conductor from anywhere on the stage.

9. Billy Budd, Act I, scene 1, seen from a fly gallery 38 feet above the stage floor.

1

2

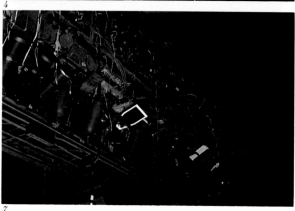

4

5

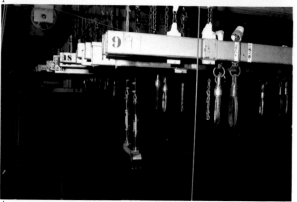

7

8

3

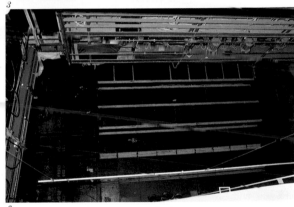

6

9

Setting the Stage

There is rarely a day during the Met's New York season that doesn't find the stage filled with scenery, a rehearsal in progress. Rehearsals with piano and skeleton scenery, full-dress rehearsals with lights, makeup, wigs, costumes, scenery, props, and rehearsals with only the scenery and lights and no performers fill the schedule. All this in addition to seven performances a week.

The scenery is designed to make the shift from rehearsal to performance and back to the next morning's rehearsal feasible. But the design is not enough. An army of stage hands—carpenters, electricians, prop men—set the stage. Often thousands of pieces are needed to create a scene. The scenery comes from the warehouses in parts to be assembled into units and larger pieces in the C-level storage area. Drops are sorted and hung, props are checked. Everything is examined, repaired and repainted, if necessary. As rehearsals proceed, lights, details and decoration are added. With the contributions of the final wardrobe, wig and makeup crews the picture is completed.

The stage manager is responsible for coordinating all action on the stage. During rehearsals and performances he "runs the show," calling cues and entrances. By the time a production is on the main stage, the stage manager has a thorough working knowledge of its requirements. He has attended many early rehearsals to familiarize himself with the production as it develops, gathering information which becomes the preliminary set of cues for the first onstage rehearsal. These cues are later refined. The efficiency of the stage manager and crew make the exhausting pattern of rehearsing and performing possible. There is no other opera house in the world with such a demanding schedule—seven performances and five rehearsals on the main stage each week.

Met stagehands are used to the technically complicated job of handling "frames" for such scenes as the magnificent armory in the third act of Otello *(above). This photograph was taken while the stage was being set.*

There are various ways of marking the stage floor in order to position the sets exactly. Here are two examples of the stage crew's technique: the marking may be done with tape (left) or nails may be pounded into the floor (right) as markers.

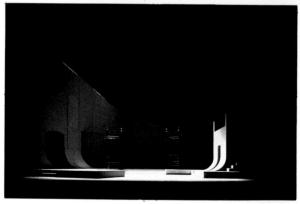

A technical rehearsal on the set (above). This was the Carmen *Goeran Gentele had planned for the opening of his first season as general manager. After his sudden death, the brilliant production became his memorial.*

Carmen, *design and realization. The model set (left) by Josef Svoboda, Czech "scenographer," his preferred title, for the Met's 1972 production. It is a stylized conception, with lights emphasizing the hot glaring Seville sun.*

The Productions

There is general inspection before every performance. The wardrobe mistress verifies the rows of costumes, the prop department double-checks to see if everything is on hand. Offstage right, in his console near the curtain line, is the stage manager who is in general charge. He has closed-circuit television on the conductor and stage; he also controls the main gold curtain. His prompt book is a score between whose pages blank sheets were bound on which he listed all cues—a permanent record of each production. Beside him sits his assistant, with a microphone to the dressing rooms, from which he calls artists, chorus and ballet. When an opera is to begin he has his eye on the clock, waiting for the second hand to reach the top. Then, the conductor on the podium, he gives the signal. "Curtain!"
The house darkens. The conductor, in the orchestra pit, bows to applause. The audience, quiet, expectant, waits to enjoy a work it may have heard a dozen or two dozen times before. Many know the opera almost by heart, through long exposure to authoritative records and to the Met's Saturday afternoon radio broadcasts and its telecasts. Though the knowledge lends depth to the enjoyment, that opening moment remains magic, an entrance to another world, a world of fantasy and mystery and vocal excitement, a world where theater and music unite in that unique art form called opera.
The productions shown on the following pages will give a glimpse of the rich variety offered by the Metropolitan Opera.

Britten's Billy Budd, *first seen in September 1978, was a triumph for all. John Dexter as director, William Dudley as designer, Raymond Leppard as conductor, David Stivender as chorus master. The cast included Peters Pears as Captain Vere, Richard Stilwell as Billy, James Morris as master-at-arms Claggart. The multi-level set of the British naval vessel (opposite) could be raised, lowered or moved, to focus on brig, captain's cabin, lower deck, or upper with its guns.*

Wagner's Tannhäuser *(overleaf) remains a glory in the production of Otto Schenk, first seen in December 1977. Sets and projections were created by Günther Schneider-Siemssen, costumes by Patricia Zipprodt, lighting by Gil Wechsler. James Levine conducted. Featured were Leonie Rysanek as Elisabeth, Grace Bumbry as Venus, James McCracken in the title role and Bernd Weikl as Wolfram. The beech trees and rolling hills of the Valley of the Wartburg evoke the actual landscape of Thuringia. The sets, using the Met's stage imaginatively to suggest vast spaces and long perspectives, glowed with German romanticism.*

The Met's latest Bohème *(second overleaf) was designed and directed by Franco Zeffirelli. Its sets invariably evoke applause and cheers from the audience. In Act II, Christmas Eve in the Latin Quarter, a crowd of almost 300 merrymakers fills the split level stage, connected by wide steps with the Café Momus below.*

Montserrat Caballé

Luciano Pavarotti

Joan Sutherland

Shirley Verrett

Marilyn Horne

Leontyne Price

Birgit Nilsson

Placido Domingo

Tatiana Troyanos

Montserrat Caballé in the title role of Cilea's **Adriana Lecouvreur.**

Luciano Pavarotti in one of his favourite roles, the simple villager Nemorino in Donizetti's Elisir d'Amore. He finally wins his love Adina, sung by Judith Blegen.

Joan Sutherland in a characteristic bel canto role, Elvira in Bellini's **Puritani.**

Shirley Verrett, beautiful as Puccini's **Tosca.**

Marilyn Horne as the shipwrecked Isabella in Rossini's Italiana in Algeri.

Leontyne Price as Verdi's Aida, a part she made her own.

Birgit Nilsson as Strauss' Elektra, one of her greatest roles.

Placido Domingo as the romantic Des Grieux in Puccini's **Manon Lescaut.**

Tatiana Troyanos as Octavian in Strauss' **Rosenkavalier.**

Sherrill Milnes in one of his most famous Verdi roles, Iago in Otello.

Overleaf
Puccini's Manon Lescaut in 1980 with Renata Scotto in the title role. This opulently realistic production was directed by Gian Carlo Menotti, sets and costumes by Desmond Heeley; Levine conducted, Placido Domingo sang Des Grieux. Poulenc's Dialogues of the Carmelites, a great and unexpected success in 1977, directed by John Dexter, sets by David Reppa, costumes by Jane Greenwood, conducted by Michel Plasson. A stark, innovative production, the opening shows the raked stage in the shape of a huge white cross with the prostrate figures of the black-habited nuns. Kurt Weill's Mahagonny, a bitter masterpiece of the Berlin twenties, came to the Met in 1979 with Teresa Stratas as the prostitute Jenny. Levine conducted, Dexter directed, sets and costumes were by Jocelyn Herbert. Alban Berg's Lulu was

first heard (1977) in the customary incomplete version but returned (1980) in its completed three-act version. Levine conducted, Dexter directed, Jocelyn Herbert did sets and costumes. Satie's ballet Parade opened the Met's French Trilogy in 1981. The dazzling poster-art sets were by David Hockney, director Dexter, conductor Manuel Rosenthal. Commedia dell'arte figures linked the ballet with the Poulenc and Ravel works which followed. Smetana's Bartered Bride, after a 36-year absence, came back to the Met in 1978, sung in English, with Jon Vickers in an unusual role for him—the stuttering Vasek. Also shown: Jean Kraft as Háta, John Cheek as Micha. Stunning in porcelain-blue and white, Le Rossignol, December 1981, was part of the Stravinsky centenary production designed by David Hockney, and directed by John Dexter. The "Nightingale" and "Fisherman," choreographed by Fredrick Ashton, were danced by Natalia Makarova and Anthony Dowell. Also part of the triple bill were Le Sacre du Printemps, and Oedipus Rex. Humperdinck's Hansel and Gretel is the perennial Christmas delight at the Met. The magical production opening in 1967 was directed by Nathaniel Merrill, designed by Robert O'Hearn. In the final scene, shown here, the witch's oven explodes, she is baked into a huge gingerbread figure, the gingerbread children come back to life and all rejoice. Verdi's Aida passed its 600 mark at the Met in 1976. Conducted by Levine, directed by Dexter, sets by David Reppa, costumes by Peter J. Hall. Here, in the Triumphal Scene, are Leontyne Price as Aida, James Morris as the Egyptian King, Bonaldo Giaiotti as Ramfis, Marilyn Horne as Amneris.

Sherrill Milnes

117

Manon Lescaut

Dialogues of the Carmelites

Lulu

Parade

Le Rossignol

Hansel and Gretel

Mahagonny

Bartered Bride

Aida

The Met's Millions

When the Metropolitan opened in October 1883, Wagner had been dead less than a year, Verdi was still alive. *Otello* and *Falstaff* were yet to come but *Trovatore, Traviata,* and *Rigoletto* were features of the first month's repertory. Wagner, too, was already entrenched. *Lohengrin* came the first season; *Tannhäuser, Die Walküre, Rienzi,* and *Die Meistersinger* during the second and third. For more than half a century the Metropolitan continued to expand its repertory and to bring to it the great singers of the day. Its fame spread but its audiences, except for the annual tours, remained the same, limited to New Yorkers for whom the Metropolitan was their pride and pleasure. Eventually the breakthrough came: radio, then television—the marvels through which opera from the Metropolitan was to be brought into homes across the nation, eventually to millions around the world.

Radio was first. Since December 7, 1940, under the sponsorship of Texaco, the Met's Saturday afternoon performances have been broadcast throughout this country and Canada. First Milton Cross and now Peter Allen is known as "the voice of the Metropolitan." An important by-product of these broadcasts are the fund-raising Historic Broadcast Recordings Series which preserves great Metropolitan Opera performances of the past.

Live from the Met television on a continuing basis dates back to that famous *Bohème* of 1977, which established a new audience record for opera on the air. Since then there have been regular telecasts each season from the Met, ranging from opera by Mozart, Verdi, and Puccini to Smetana, Weill, and Berg. With *Manon Lescaut* in 1980 a new era began: the Metropolitan became available world-wide. Visitors from out-of-town and abroad now approach the Metropolitan with a feeling of recognition, coupled with a certain awe. They enter its doors with expectation. They might be echoing Elisabeth's words in *Tannhäuser: "Dich, teure Halle . . ."* "Dear, precious Hall, joyfully I greet you, beloved place."

Cameraman (above) filming a "Live from the Met" telecast. The TV monitor just under him shows the live action on stage.

Luciano Pavarotti and Renata Scotto (opposite) in La Bohème, *the final scene when Mimi, dying, has returned to the garret in the Latin Quarter where she first met Rodolfo. This La Bohème was the first "Live from the Met" telecast on March 15, 1977. It drew an unprecedented audience of 7,655,000.*

Leonie Rysanek (overleaf) as Elisabeth in Tannhäuser, *behind her is John Macurdy as the Landgrave; Renata Scotto (second overleaf) in the title role of* Manon Lescaut.

Appendix

House Statistics

Overall Dimensions:	Length: 451' Width: 175' at front, 234' at back Height: 96' Ten stories (6 above ground, ground level, 3 below)
Exterior Materials:	Travertine: 42,000 cubic feet Glass: 156 panels
Interior:	Red carpet: 8,000 sq. yds. (2,000 in auditorium) Burgundy velour wall coverings: 3,000 sq. yds. Crystal chandeliers: 32; main chandelier in auditorium 17' diameter
Auditorium:	873,000 cubic feet Length: 90' (stage apron to box face) Height: 72' (auditorium floor to ceiling) Ceiling: 4,000 rolls of 23 carat gold leaf
Curtain:	1,000 sq. yds. gold silk damask
Seats:	3,800 chairs, vary from 19" to 23" wide to conform to "three-row vision" sequence
Orchestra pit:	26½' wide 90' long motorized podium
Seating and Standing Room:	Total seating & standing capacity for opera: 4,065 (35 additional seats when smaller orchestra is used for ballet presentations only)
Fly Galleries: (left and right)	Five galleries ranging in height from 38' to gallery 1 to 101'6" to gallery 5
Rigging for Lighting:	Four fixed light bridges and 9 border lights

Main Stage Statistics

Overall Dimensions:	Width: 230'0" (right side wall to left side wall) Depth: 148'0"
Architectural Proscenium:	Width: 54'0" Height: 54'0"
Black Proscenium:	(incl. tormentors and bridge) (Designates zero/setting line on stage) 8'0" upstage of architectural proscenium
Left and right tormentors:	(Used in tandem w/#1 lighting bridge) Variable Width: 44'0"–54'0"
#1 Lighting Bridge:	(teaser) Variable Height: 0'0"–40'6"

Main Stage Area:	Width: 101′0″
	Depth: 80′0″ (from architectural proscenium)
	Maximum height: 110′10″ to bottom of 1st gridiron
Right Side Stage:	1′0″ above main stage floor
	Width: 60′0″
	Depth: 48′0″
	Height: 29′6″ (maximum overhead clearance)
Left Side Stage:	1′0″ above main stage floor
	Width: 60′0″
	Depth: 40′0″
	Height: 29′6″ (maximum overhead clearance)
Upstage or Rear Wagon:	1′0″ above main stage floor
	Width: 60′0″
	Depth: 60′0″
Turntable:	Diameter: 57′0″
Hydraulic Stage Elevators:	One equalizer for rear wagon and seven elevators
Equalizer:	(hydraulic elevator used only in conjunction with the downstage extension of the rear wagon)
	Width: 46′0″
	Depth: 4′0″
	Equalizer travels: stage level to (− 1′0″)
Elevators (Lifts):	Seven, each at
	Width: 60′0″
	Depth: 8′0″
Stage Traps:	Total of fifty located in decks of lifts
Each trap:	3′5″ Wide
	4′0″ Deep
Stage Rigging:	109 house pipes or line sets. Pipes are spaced 4″–7″ on center and connected to electric motor winches.
Loading Capacity:	1000 lbs. per pipe
Cycloramas:	Two, rolled for storage–one blue and one white
Each cyclorama:	270′0″ Wide
	109′0″ High
Rigging for Lighting:	Fixed light bridges and border lights
Act Curtains:	
The Gold Curtain:	Gold patterned silk damask, tableau drape
Gold Curtain speeds:	1) Fast: 7–11 sec.
	2) Slow: 12 sec.–2 min.
"Guillotine Curtain"*:	Gold velour, just upstage of the Gold Curtain which is flown out when Guillotine is used.
Guillotine speed:	0′0″–180′/min.
	* So called because curtain is flown vertically from house pipe

Dedication

Andrew Kershaw: Hungarian-born, English-educated, British commando, émigré to Canada, chairman of a great U.S. advertising agency, and lover of opera. That is how the memorial plaque should read. Each biographic tidbit leads us to the real description of the man and the reason his friends have contributed funds for this book as a memorial to Andrew's memory. Because of his passion for opera, Andrew loved the Metropolitan Opera and served as a managing director of the Metropolitan Opera Association and a member of the Board of Directors of the Metropolitan Opera Guild for a number of years.

He was a tough, analytical, and successful businessman who used all his mercantile disciplines to help his beloved opera company. He believed that was the least he could do in return for the hours of joy and freedom he felt after the curtain rose at the Metropolitan Opera House. As Katharine O'Neil, president of the Metropolitan Opera Guild, wrote in remembrance of Andrew, "To the Metropolitan Opera Guild, Andrew Kershaw brought a new and forward-looking spirit which rejuvenated it and reawakened its sense of purpose."

So, this book is a natural extension, reminding us of his good work for the opera. But it is also meant to be a recognition for the rest of us that success without song, toughness without a sense of human drama and sadness, and an analytical mind without a passion for art makes for an empty soul.

Andrew Kershaw's soul was filled to the brim!